MW01688698

LOOM KNITTING FOR BEGINNERS

Step by Step Guide for Novice Knitters

Table of Content

INTRODUCTION

You probably know that you can knit with needles and weave with a loom, but have you ever tried knitting with a loom? Not only is it possible, but loom knitting is a fast and fun way to create all kinds of beautifully knit items.

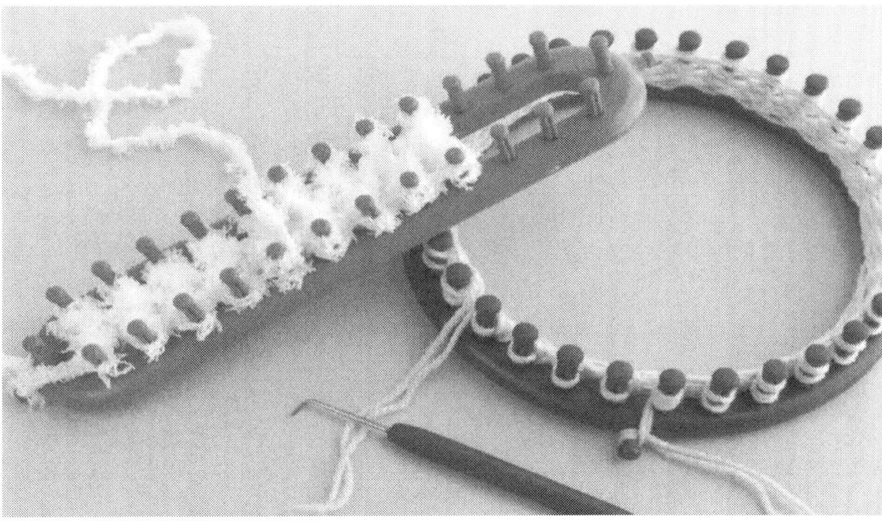

Learning the basics of loom knitting is an easy way to get started and it's a great way to introduce kids to this craft. With just a few simple steps they can see the knitted material forming! But this isn't only for children. Knitting on a loom can produce the same types of projects that traditional knitting can, including intricate designs like cables. The benefit to making these on a loom is that it's often easier on your hands and it usually works up faster.

Loom knitting has been around for hundreds, maybe

thousands, of years. The most reliable information dates back to the 16th century, when someone was looking to create an alternative method of knitting and a framed knitting "machine" was born. If you've ever tried finger knitting or spool knitting, you'll see the connection, which may even be how this larger form of knitting on a loom came to be.

Easy on the hands, loom knitting is the craft technique of using a loom instead of needles to create beautiful knitted fabric, which can be transformed into sublime homeware, fashions and cosy accessories. While using a loom might look fiddly business, loom knitting is surprisingly easy when you know how, and is even great for kids!

In this beginner's loom knitting guide i'll introduce you to the wonderful world of knitting looms, give you a tour of some essential stitches and even get you started on your first pattern. Unlock the joys of going needleless!

WHAT IS KNITTING LOOM?

The iconic 'loom', which simply refers to the crafty contraption used to weave together yarn (or thread) to produce fabric, has widespread origins from Europe in the Middle Ages to the intricate craftwork of the Amerindian tribes of the Americas.

Today, loom knitting remains a celebrated technique that can be used to create anything from gorgeous wall hangings, hats, scarfs, blankets and beyond!

Loom knitting is especially brilliant for those who experience sore hands, such as those with arthritis or carpal tunnel syndrome. It's also a wonderful alternative for those who simply favour a needleless approach to their projects, not to mention that the technique is incredibly fast so you can whip up marvellous creations in record time. With a variety of knitting looms and a broad spectrum of techniques available, loom knitting provides the basis to create diverse and showstopping projects. But first, let's talk looms.

CHOOSING YOUR KNITTING LOOM

There are many varieties of loom available depending of the project you're embarking on. While rake (long) looms are excellent for flat panel projects such as blankets, circular looms are joyously compatible with hats and cowls. Here are some of the types of loom you are likely to encounter on your loom knitting adventure!

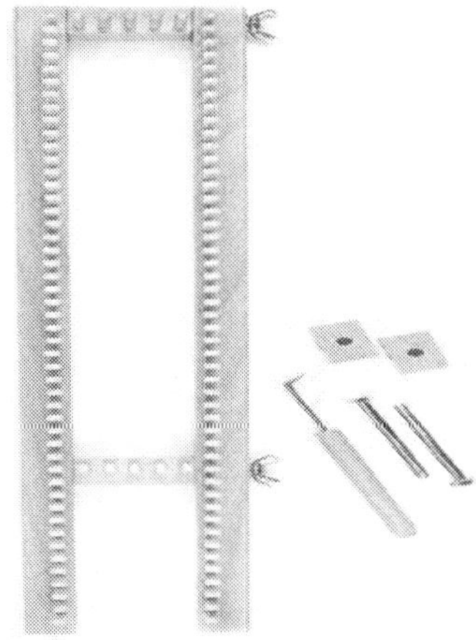

Rake looms

Rake looms, also known as long looms, are characterised by a single row of pegs, generally used to create flat panel projects such as blankets and scarves from single knitting. When two rakes are set aside one another you then have what as known as a knitting board. Some rake looms on the market may include two rows with an additional peg on either end of the loom allowing you to work in the round if you so wish. Just like regular knitting, fabric produced from a simple rake loom will have a knit side and purl side. The gauge of the long knitting loom is determined by the distance between each pin, so the closer together your pins the finer your knitted fabric!

Circular and other round looms

Round knitting looms refer to a loom where there is no

stopping point, unlike its cousin the rake. A round knitting loom is any device where you can continuously weave, this might appear in a menagerie of wonderful shapes and sizes, including circular, oval, square, triangular and even heart-shaped looms.

Round loom knitting projects are often (but not exclusively) tubular shaped because of ability to continuously knit in the round, which means if you're looking to make socks, sleeves or cowls, or anything that might have a tube or circle shape - round looms are a must!

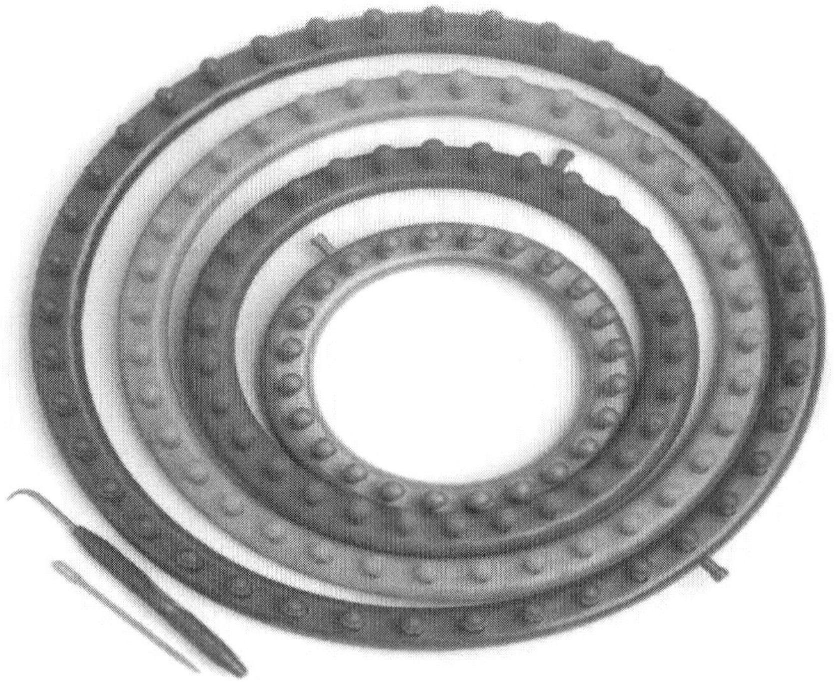

S-loom, or the serenity loom, has an 'infinity' figure of

eight structure, and is the perfect knitting loom for crafting large panels of fabric which can be sewn together to create dreamy afghans and blankets.

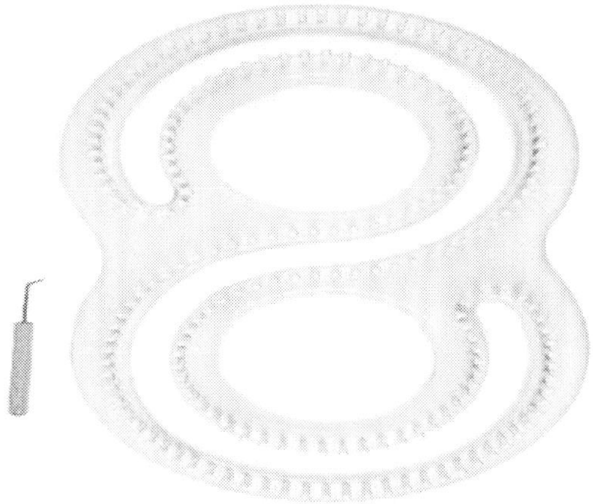

Sock looms

Sock looms include an adjustable gauge so you can easily create increases and decreases to knit the perfect size for your whole family, whether you're creating grown up socks or baby booties.

Weaving Loom

Loom weaving is a fibre craft that is distinctive from loom knitting. The weaving loom, unlike knitting loom, doesn't have pegs and instead facilitates a series of warped threads, that you can use as a framework to weave in your yarn.

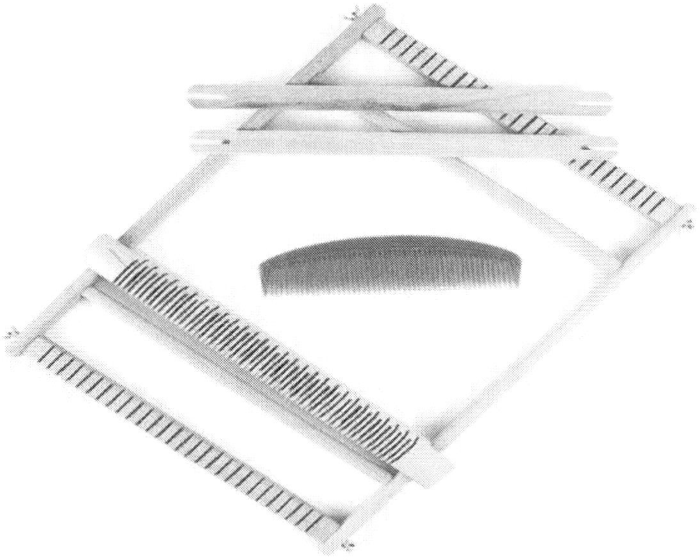

The weaving loom produces stunning wall hangings and tapestry. If loom weaving tickles your fancy why not try your hand at this wall hanging tutorial.

HOW TO LOOM KNIT?

Your favourite knitting stitches can be created on your loom according to how you wrap the yarn around the pegs. Different wrapping techniques will produce different textures and designs to produce satisfyingly plush projects from traditional stitches to more intricate styles including lace or cablework. Anything is possible with a loom and a little know-how!

It's important to bear in mind often loom knitting stitches have different names to those created by needles.

HOW TO USE A KNITTING LOOM?

Knitting looms come in a variety of shapes and sizes depending on what kind of project you are making. While long looms work best for projects like scarves, round (or circular) looms are best for hats, socks or anything that has a tube structure.

BASE, PETS AND GAUGE

Let's get down to basics. The anatomy of a loom is made up of three essential components; base, pegs and gauge. The base is the frame at the bottom of your loom which might be a long or round available in lots of sizes. The pegs describe the multiple short pins attached to the base - sometimes these are just called pins. The gauge is the distance between each peg (or pin), the wider the gap is between the pegs the greater the gauge. Easy-peasy!

WHAT DETERMINE THE SIZE OF YOUR PROJECT?

The size of your project can be affected by many things, the first is the size of your loom. Many fledgling loom knitters refer to the size of the loom as the number of pegs, but this is a massive no-no! As a beginner it's important to remember that it's actually the size of the base that determines the size of your project, not necessarily the number of pegs. The number of pegs and the gauge influence the tension of your stitches, or how tightly knit together your stitches are. More pegs does not necessarily mean a bigger size.

Saying that, there is one exception - and that is the style of stitch. If you use a loose stitch such as an Ewrap stitch then your fabric will be looser and therefore be a slightly bigger size then if you were to use a garter stitch on your loom.

Row vs peg count

When it comes to the number of rows and pegs on your

loom knitting project, it's important to remember that these are not interchangeable. The peg count determines the circumference or width of your project, and the number of rows is how many times you repeat this. If you are making a tubular project such as socks or a hat on a round loom, then the rows will only add to the length of the tube, but not give anymore give around the foot or head.

In addition to your loom and yarn you will also need a hook to catch and pull your loops of yarn over to create the knitted stitches.

Loom knitting stitches

Just like knitting with needles, loom knitting includes a whole encyclopedia of stitches to craft beautifully textured knitwear.

Before we get to specific stitches, there are two fundamental methods of knitting on a loom: single and double knitting.

Single knitting

Single-knitting is when you knit stitches on pegs next to one another, creating a fabric which will have a 'right' and 'wrong' side.

Knit stitch (k)

The knit stitch on a loom has the very same texture and

look as a knit stitch created using regular needles. The knit stitch is achieved by using your hook to pull at the yarn looped around your peg, to create a new loop. By lifting the old loop up and over, you replace with the new loop on your peg to create a new knit stitch. And that's it!

This is the primal stitch that once mastered can be combined with purl to create garter stitch or even ribbed stitches.

Flat stitch (f)

Flat stitch is a close cousin of knit stitch, except it's tighter more compact. Stretch the working yarn across the top loop of the peg and simply use your hook to lift the bottom loop over and off your peg, securing the working yarn in place by making it a new loop.

Purl stitch (p)

Just like in traditional knitting, the purl stitch is the reverse of the knit stitch, meaning that the backside of your fabric will be knit material the frontside will be purl. Both knit and purl stitches are fantastic starting points to launch you into a world of glorious textures and designs as you learn to loom knit.

Double knitting

Double-knitting is when you knit across two rails, if you are using a long loom, so you have a front and a back peg, meaning you get the same texture on both sides of your fabric.

No wrap stitch (nw)

In loom knitting this might be referred to as a flat (stockinette) stitch, and when knitting with needles this is known as the basic knit stitch (k). Just like the gorgeous basic fabric produced when knitting with needles, the no wrap stitch creates sturdy yet beautifully adaptable material which can be transformed into fabulous accessories and homeware. As one of the most basic stitches, the no wrap stitch is a staple for the avid loom knitter and can be used on a long loom or round one. And that's a wrap!

EWrap (ew)

Better known as the twisted stockinette stitch when knitting with needles (tw St st), the ewrap works a treat on both long and round looms.

Single ribbed stitch or ribbing stitch (rib)

Perfect for gloves and garments with the iconic ribbed effect, the single ribbed stitch sees ewrap stitches alternate with purl stitches on each row creating glorious ridges of yarn.

TYPES OF KNITTING LOOM

Knitting looms come in different shapes, sizes, and materials, and go by a variety of names such as a *knitting board, rake, frame,* or the classic *loom.* Some have a set number of pegs, while others are adjustable.

You can even make your own!

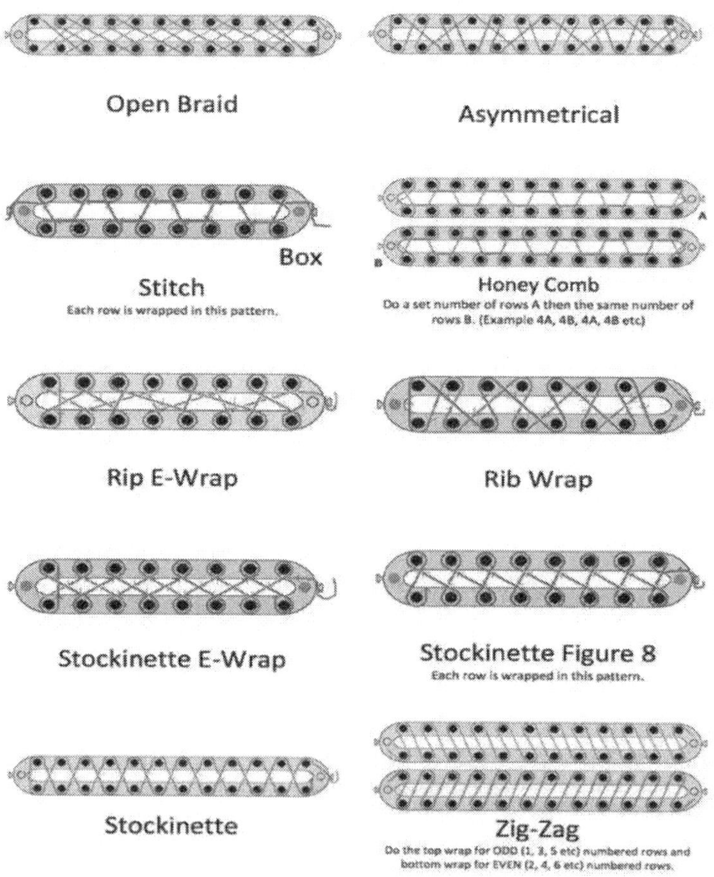

Just as knitting needles come in different thicknesses, which determine the size or gauge of your knitting, the peg size and spacing on knitting looms also determine the gauge. Larger pegs spaced farther apart make bulky or open knitting, while thinner pegs spaced more closely result in finer or tighter knitting.

Each peg on a loom holds one stitch, so the number of pegs also makes a difference. You don't have to use every peg for a project, but you do need to have enough to achieve the size of the knitted piece you want. For example, to make a blanket without joining several pieces together, you would need many pegs, which you find on looms shaped like a large S or figure 8.

Because the loom size and shape is so important to the outcome of the knitting, it's crucial to check that you have the correct loom for a project. Patterns typically tell what type of loom to use, along with peg count and spacing. It's also important to pay attention to the yarn weight recommended for a pattern or loom, including whether to hold more than one strand of yarn together.

HOW LOOM KNITTING WORKS

Most loom knitting falls into three categories: circular knitting, which forms a tube; single knitting, which forms a single panel; and double knitting, which forms a reversible, extra thick fabric. Different types of looms help make this possible.

You can do single knitting on any type of loom, while circular knitting requires a continuous ring or frame of pegs. If you have a round loom but want to make a flat (non-tube) piece of knitting, simply work back and forth on the pegs instead of going around in a circle.

Both single and circular knitting usually begin with an e-wrap cast on, which wraps the yarn around each peg you are using for your project. The process of wrapping remains the same as you add more rows or rounds of stitches.

Long looms with double rows of pegs are for double knitting. (Some have a peg at each end so you can use them for circular knitting, and you can also always use these for single knitting.) Double knitting starts with a figure 8 cast-on, wrapping the yarn back and forth across the rows of pegs, which continues as you knit.

When doing single and double knitting, you can adjust the size of your project by working on only one portion of the loom. That's harder to do with circular knitting, which needs evenly spaced pegs for all the stitches.

After wrapping yarn once around all the pegs, it's time to wrap it a second time. Next, use a knitting hook (which comes with most looms) to lift the bottom loop of yarn up and over the peg, leaving the top loop in place. This completes a knit stitch. After lifting all the bottom loops over the pegs, you start again, wrapping the pegs and making new stitches.

You can also learn how to make other types of stitches such as traditional purl stitches, loom-knitting-exclusive stitches, and cast-on and bind-off methods to craft patterns and shapes in your work.

1. An Infinity Scarf

This infinity scarf is a quick and easy knitting project

that you can do on a rectangular or round loom - whatever you have around!

I've been working on this pattern for a couple weeks, and now I've streamlined the process enough you should be able to have a totally finished infinity scarf in 3-4 hours. The scarf pictured here came in just under three hours, but I think I've gotten super quick at it since it's the third one I've made in a week. ;)

Materials Needed

- 2 skeins of chunky yarn - I used Lion Brand Hometown USA yarns for these - the yarn pictured here is Cheyenne Wild Iris
- knitting loom with at least 20 pegs (this is the set I'm using!)
- yarn needle
- loom hook
- scissors
- measuring tape

The scarves shown in this instructable are made on 15 pegs and are 40-50 inches of knitting long. If you choose to use variegated yarn, you'll have just enough for the scarf with two skeins - around 130 yards of yarn. If you choose a solid yarn you'll have closer to 160 yards of yarn per two skeins, so you can increase the number of pegs to 20 and keep the length of the knitting between 40-50 inches to make a thicker scarf.

Step 1: Anchor Your Work With a Slipknot

This will depend on the sort of loom you have.

Either place the slipknot on the horizontal peg on a round loom, or on a vertical peg to the left or right of where you'd like to knit on a rectangular or straight loom.

Step 2: Loop the Pegs Twice

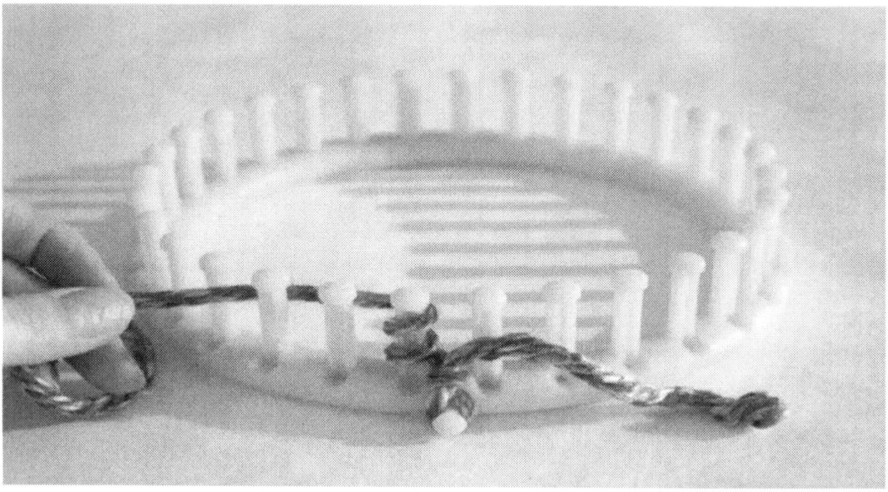

Going to the left or right of the peg with the slipknot, (whichever feels best for you - I'm left handed so I'm going to move to the left!) loop 15 pegs twice each.

Hold the yarn taut when you reach the end.

Step 3: Bring the Bottom Loop on Each Peg Over the Top

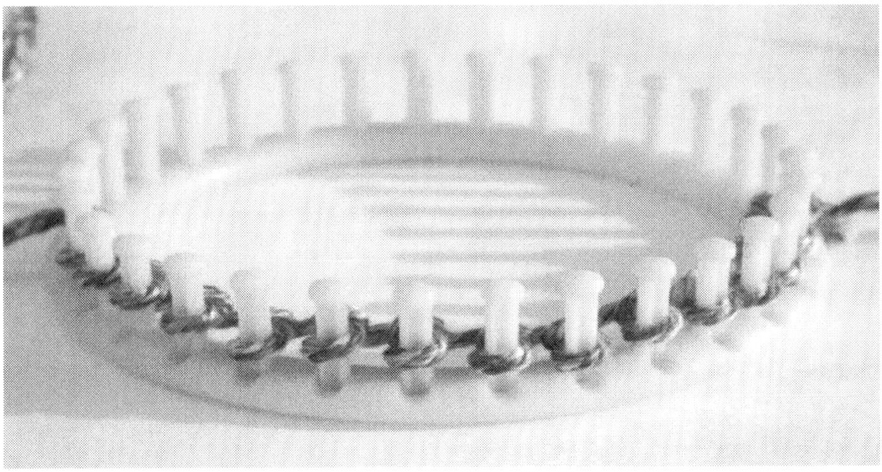

Start from the last peg you wrapped (while holding the working yarn!) and bring the bottom loop of yarn over the top one until all pegs just have one loop of yarn on them.

Step 4: Start Your First Row of Knitting

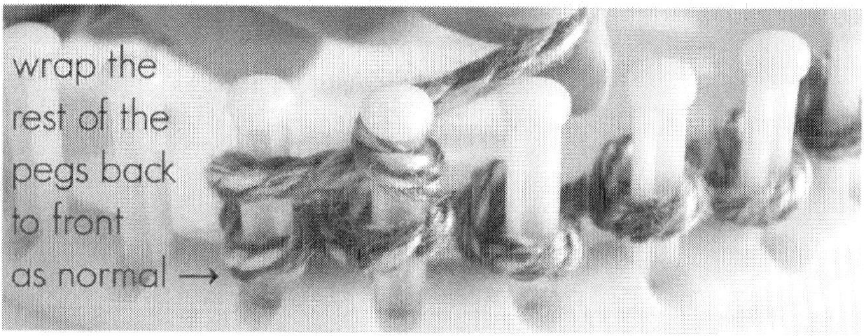

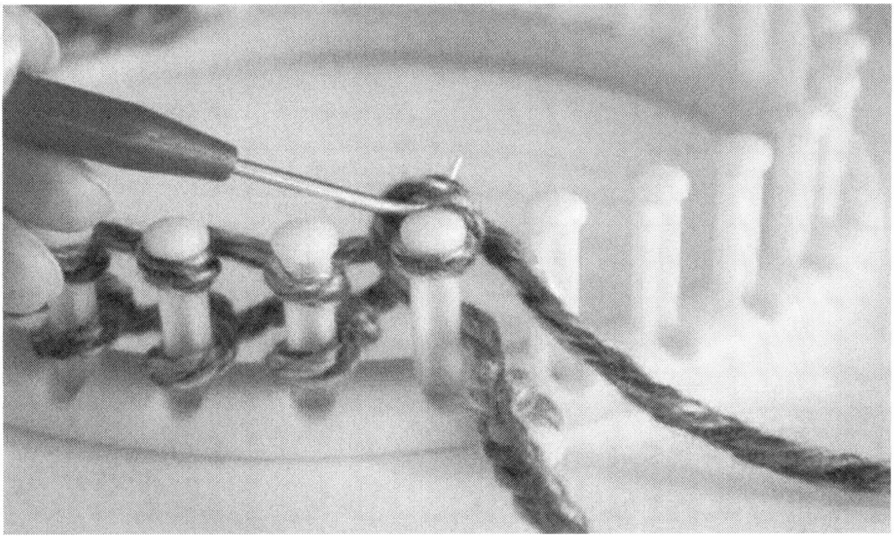

This will be just like regular loom knitting, with one difference. Whenever you start a new row of knitting, you'll wrap the first peg in the row so the yarn is just going in front of the peg, while the rest of the pegs are wrapped back to front.

If you start from the left, you'll wrap the first peg counterclockwise, and the rest clockwise. Bring the bottom yarn over on each peg.

If you start from the right, you'll wrap the first peg clockwise, and the rest counterclockwise. Bring the bottom yarn over on each peg.

Except for that one difference, just keep wrapping the pegs and looping the bottom yarn over!

Step 5: Remove the Slip Knot From the Peg You Placed It On

Once you've knit a few rows, pull the slipknot loose. Leave the yarn tail hanging free.

Leaving it intact will make the finished knitting hang off the peg, which may warp it!

Step 6: Knit and Knit Some More

Keep on knitting - go until you hit the end of the yarn! As you knit, the scarf edges will begin to curl. Let them do what they want - it makes the scarf look nice in the end. :D

Step 7: Adding the Second Skein of Yarn

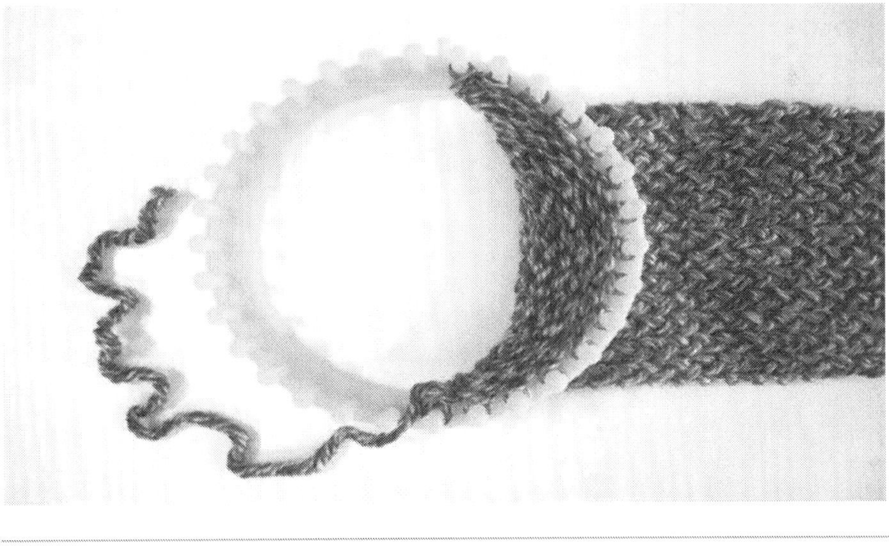

When you've knitted far enough that you're left with a tail of yarn that's not long enough to finish another row, you need to add in the second skein of yarn.

There are loads of ways to start a new skein, but I'm choosing the do this the super easy way: by tying a knot! Because I'm using a chunky yarn it's not as obvious as it would normally be.

Just tie the end of the current working yarn to the beginning of the new yarn skein using a granny knot. Pull it as tight as you can - if the knot is still moving around, keep pulling it tight until it's stationary! Once it's as tight as you can get it, cut the yarn tails off.

Step 8: Knit Until It Reaches 40-50 Inches

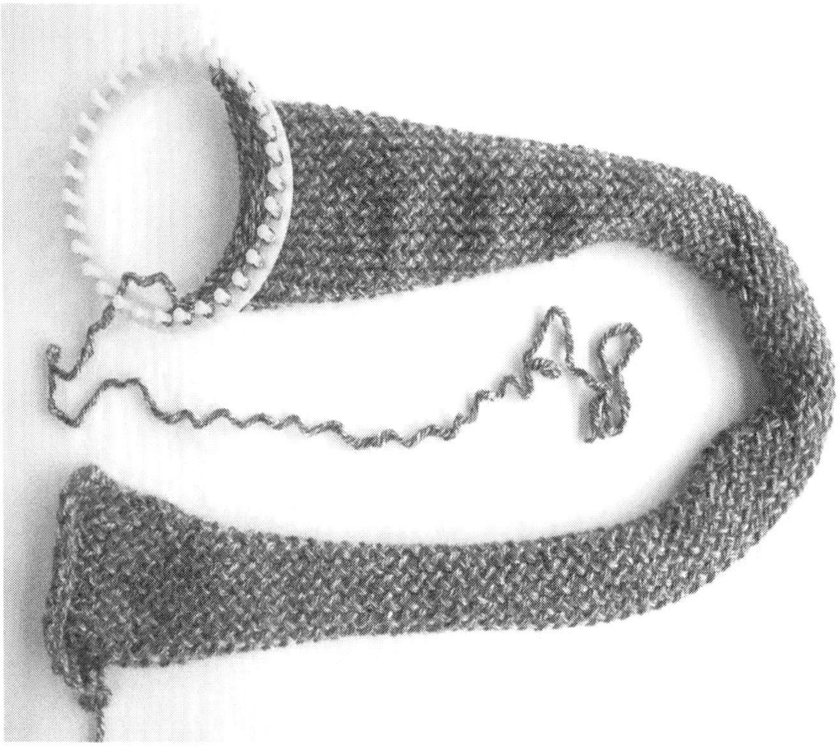

40 inches will leave you with a snugly fitting infinity scarf - 50 inches will be a bit more loose. You can awkwardly try it on while it's still on the hoop to see what works for you.

End with your yarn on the left side to follow the next steps in the easiest way! (But don't blame me when someone walks into the room and finds you trying to wrap the scarf around your neck twice and not smack yourself in the head with the hoop. I'm pretty sure my boyfriend caught me but was too nice to say how weird it was. D:)

Step 9: Loop the End of the Scarf Back Over the Pegs

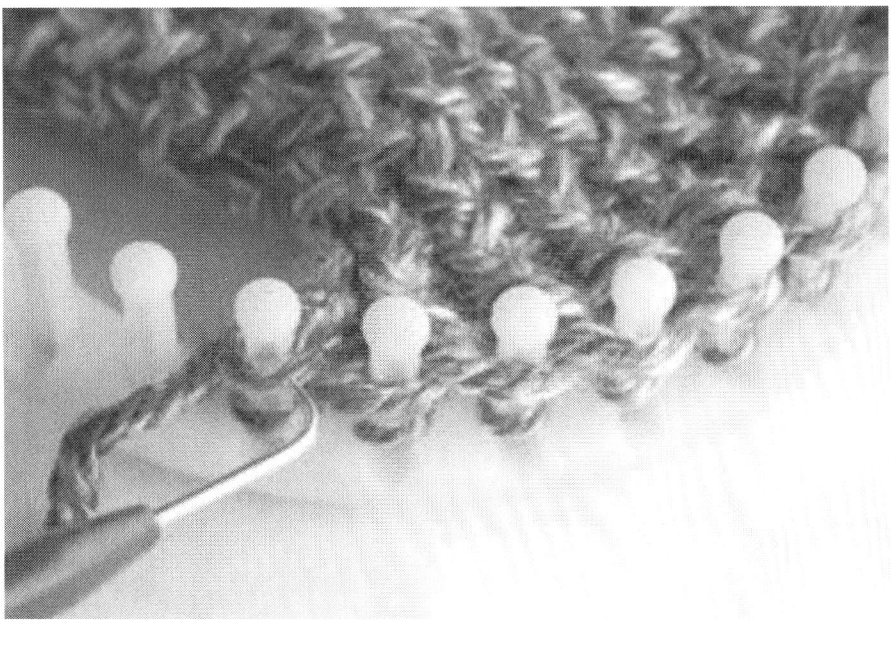

Much like the brim of the knitted hat I did, we're going to bringing the very beginning of our knitting back over the pegs.

Pull the beginning of the scarf through the hoop as shown above. Make sure it doesn't get twisted!

Now you'll want to bring the loops at the very beginning of the scarf over the pegs. It might take a couple tries to get a loop on each peg - they can be tricksy!

Keep in mind that one of the loops is a little hidden on the end next to the yarn tail from the slipknot. You might need to use the loom hook to get that one. (see picture three to see which loop I mean)

Step 10: Loop Over the Bottom Part of the Scarf

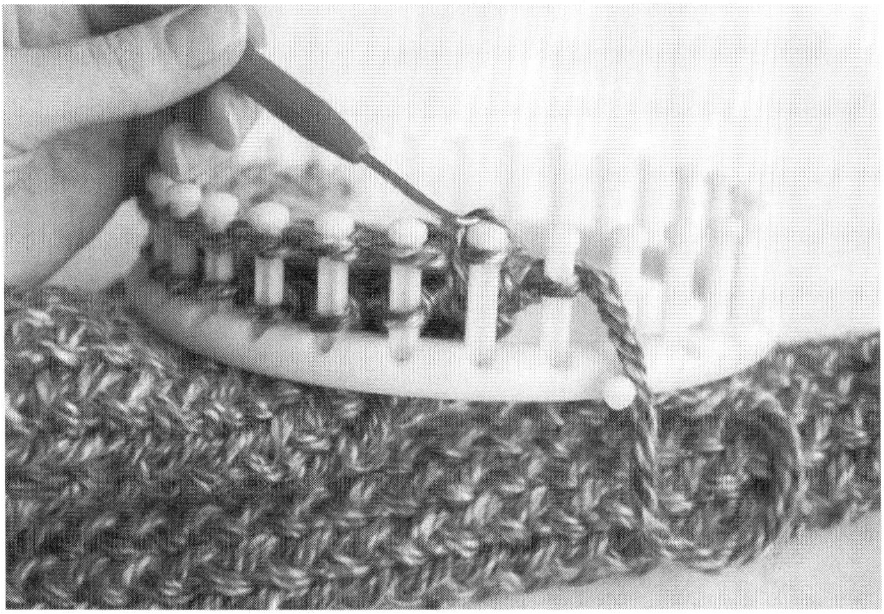

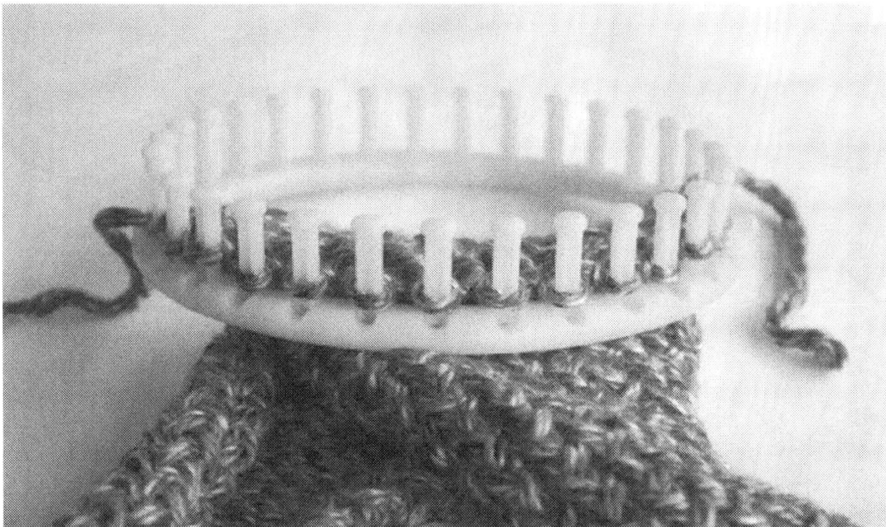

Once you have all the loops placed on the pegs, bring the bottom loops over the top so you've only got one loop on each of the pegs.

Now we'll cast off!

Step 11: Casting Off

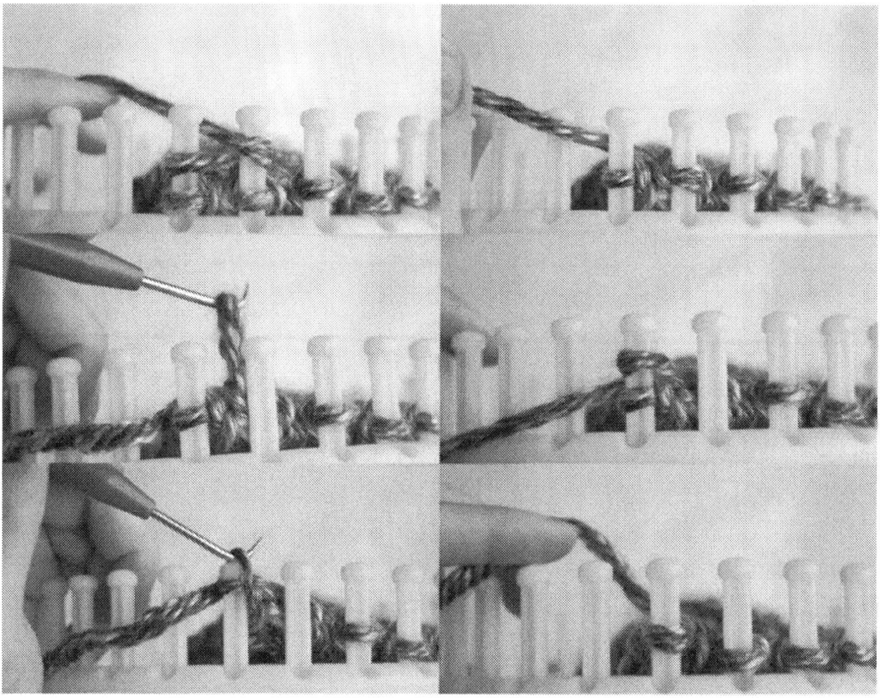

This is the best way I've seen to finish your loom knitting so it's nice and neat! We're essentially going to work on two pegs at a time, looping and removing the loops to the right as we go.

I highly recommend checking out this video by the awesome Sophia Burns to see it in action. It might help my photos and explanation make better sense. :)

Here are the basic steps:

1. Starting from the left, wrap the first peg

counterclockwise and the second peg clockwise.

2. Bring the bottom loops over the top loops on both pegs.
3. Take the loop from the second peg and put it on the first and pull the thread so it's not as loose.
4. Bring the bottom loop over the top one.
5. Take the lone loop off the first peg and transfer to the second peg.
6. Wrap the third peg clockwise.
7. Bring the bottom loop on the third peg over the top loop.
8. Transfer the loop on the third peg over to the second peg and tighten. Loop over.
9. Bring the loop left on the second peg to the third peg.
10. Repeat the wrapping, looping and transferring to the right until you're left with one peg.
11. Wrap once more and bring the bottom loop over the top one.

Now you can grab that last loop and pull it off the loom.

Keep the loop between your fingers so you know where it is. We'll tidy it up on the next step!

Check out that sweet seam you just made!! So professional. :D

Step 12: Secure the Loop

Pull at the loop so it becomes a little bigger, and slip the working yarn tail through it and pull it tight.

If you lucked out and ended up with the slipknot tail and the tail from the working yarn on the same side, knot those together.

Step 13: Weave in the Loose Ends and You're Done!

Now you'll need to weave in the loose ends with a yarn needle - both the working yarn tail from the middle seam and the short tail from the slipknot we made first thing. Thread a yarn needle with the end of the yarn and weave it into the scarf.

Try to make sure you aren't bringing the yarn through to the front of the work - keep it on the back side and make lots of tiny stitches. Tie knots when you're done - just wherever they'll be less obvious. If you have a yarn you can untwist, divide it into two sections and tie it off.

Enjoy! You just knitted a super warm and awesome scarf!

Step 13: More Photos of the Scarves

Just because I'm really proud of them :D

The black, grey and purple scarves were made 15 pegs wide, the cream scarf was made 20 pegs wide.

2. Loom-Knit Cowl

Are you still collecting ideas for handmade Christmas gifts? I have a great easy one to share with you today (yep, that's right - I said easy). I am going to share how to make a cute and simple cowl. It's not crochet, you don't need knotting needles - you can get this look by using a loom knitter. If you're not familiar with loom knitters - they are actually categorized as a kids' craft! Because truly, they are that easy! I have never picked up a crochet hook in my life (despite all the times I've promised myself to learn... maybe next year!) and I made this easy cowl in 2 hours. (I know, I usually give you one-hour projects... but this ine is truly twice as awesome, haha.)

This is a tutorial that I originally shared at the Crafts

Unleashed blog – where I contribute a couple times a month. That is the inspiration blog for consumercrafts.com. So you will notice links below to products from the Consumer Crafts Site. I am including them here to make it easy to locate supplies – I don't get any sort of referral or affiliate credit if you make a purchase, though I was provided with these materials so that I could share the tutorial at Crafts Unleashed. If you also read there (and I highly recommend it – there is some amazing creativity on the design team!) then you may already have seen this project, but I wanted to share here today in case you're still in search of a great last-minute idea!

Materials

- Knitting Loom Kit
- One Skein of Yarn (I used Lion Brand Homespun Yarn in the Edwardian color)

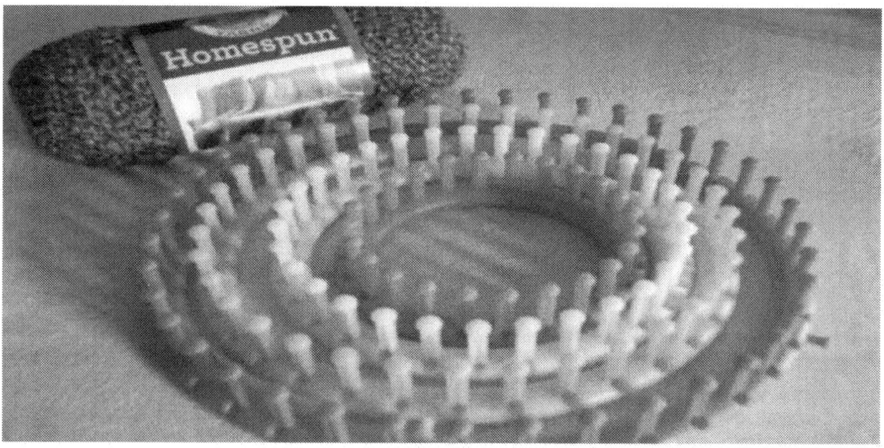

Instructions

I used the largest (pink) ring in the set because it fit easily over my head. (If you are making a child-sized cowl, you can use the next smaller ring.) These knitters also come with instructions for making a loom-knit hat, so you could certainly make a matching accessory!

Start at the peg on the side. You may find it helpful to wrap your yarn end around the side peg to secure it while you get started. Loop your yarn around each peg, making your way around the ring. Don't get your loops too tight, or they will be difficult to work with when you begin to weave. I worked in a clockwise direction through my project, but you can work in either direction you prefer - you will just need to stay consistent through the end.

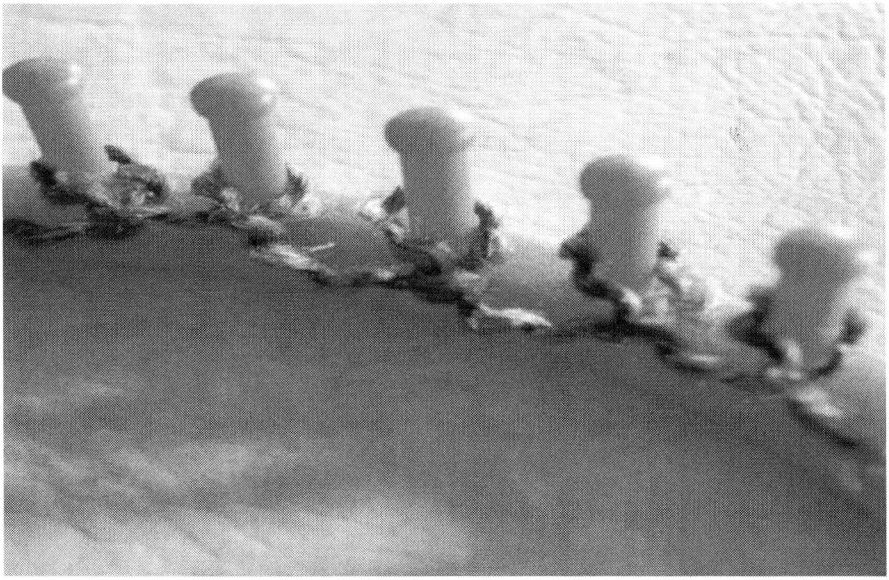

Once you complete one ring, you will need to wrap a second row before you can begin to weave. You will always be working with two rows at a time.

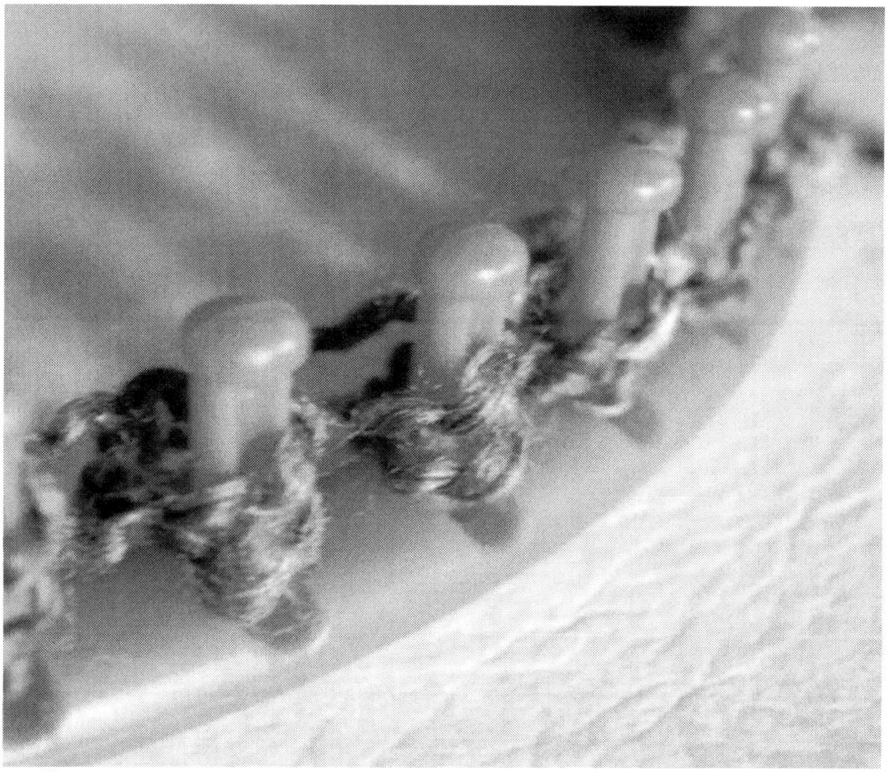

Now, you can begin weaving! From the outside of the ring, take the bottom loop, and pass it over the top loop and over the peg itself, into the center of the ring. It's easiest if you use the weaving tool included with the set, though you could also use a crochet hook or even your fingers.

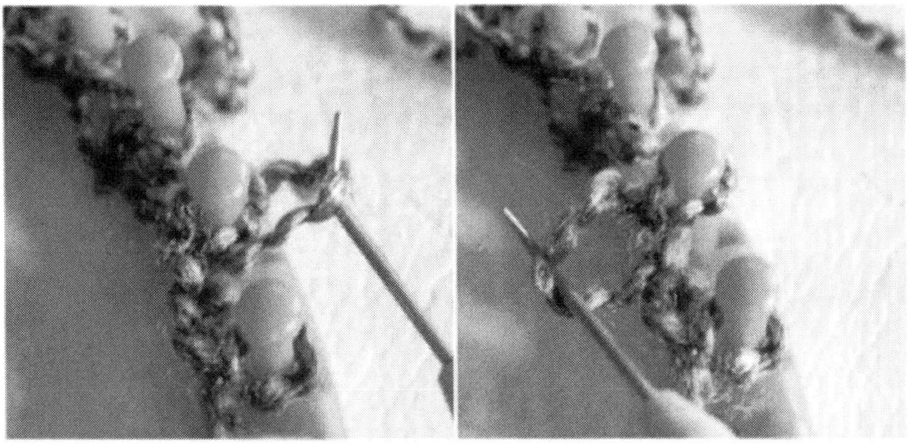

Once you work your way all the way around the ring, you have completed your first row of knitting! Loop your yarn around the pegs just as you did in the previous step, and each time you complete a row, weave it just as before, passing the bottom row over the pegs.

I knitted 30 rows for this cowl, and I used less than half a skein of yarn. I would recommend a minimum of 30 rows, though for a chunkier-looking cowl, you could easily knit double that number.

To finish your cowl when you are done knitting, unwind a length of yarn that will fit all the way around the loom with a couple of inches to spare.

Cut it off, and thread it onto the plastic needle in the kit. Beginning at the peg that marks your rows, pass the needle through the loop remaining on the peg. When you have passed the yarn through, you can slip that loop off the peg. Do this for each loop, until you have closed them all off. It's easy to make this final loop too tight, so stretch your cowl to be sure the rows are uniform. Then, tie a knot (I didn't use any special knot - just a standard double knot) to secure the end, and trim off the excess. Do the same thing for the beginning row to get rid of that excess "tail."

At this point - you will have a beautiful completed cowl! Mine took me about 2 hours from start to finish - which included getting the hang of the technique. So even a true beginner can complete this in an afternoon or an evening!

I have been wearing this cowl almost daily with all the snow we've had the past week or two here in Michigan. It's just the right weight – not too bulky to fit under a jacket or to wear on its own with a top, but it's enough to keep me feeling nice and cozy. And you better believe I'm making more as gifts this year!

So did you use a loom knitter as a kid? Are you laughing that I'm just discovering it now? I had SO much fun with this project!

3. Loom-Knit Hat

I have been bitten majorly hard with the loom knitting bug. Every once in a while this thing happens where I try a new (or new to me) craft and fall head over heels purchasing absolutely everything I might ever need that has anything to do with my new craft/hobby.

I started loom knitting while I was sick and stuck in bed. It was a good way to keep my hands busy, an absolute must for my sanity and, in this case, my health since it kept me busy with making instead of scrubbing baseboards or something equally dumb to do when ill.

Here are the reasons why I LOVE loom knitting. You can buy a knitting loom for CHEAP. You can make one cap with only 1 skein of Lion Brand Hometown USA yarn making it a CHEAP little project that you can actually give to somebody to use. If you're not sure how to make a loom knit hat to begin with, well, I've got you covered.

Still with me? Good! Let's get after it.

Materials

- Bulky yarn knitting loom (I love my Boye set)
- Hometown USA yarn (equivalent to 1 skein) – get it for around $3 apiece at Walmart, seriously the cheapest price I have found…

Instructions

Get after loom knitting your cap as you would anyway. It's time to switch business up when you have 6-8 inches of length knitted up (more or less depending on the size of your brim, I suppose).

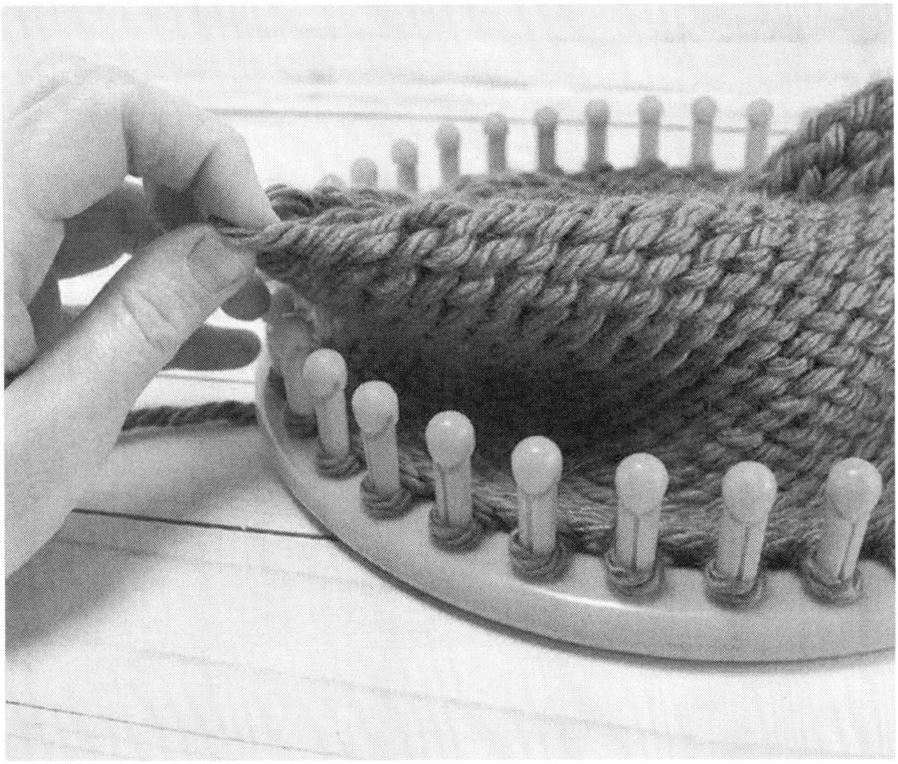

Follow down the knit from the loop on the peg to the end of the piece. Grab that loop at the end and pull it over that peg.

Working to the left, or right, continue bringing the matching bottom loop up placing it onto the peg.

This is what your piece will look like when all of the ends have been matched up. This is your brim where the knit is doubled up making it warmer and visibly thicker when worn.

To wrap this brim up bring the bottom loop over the peg, just as you would normally knit.

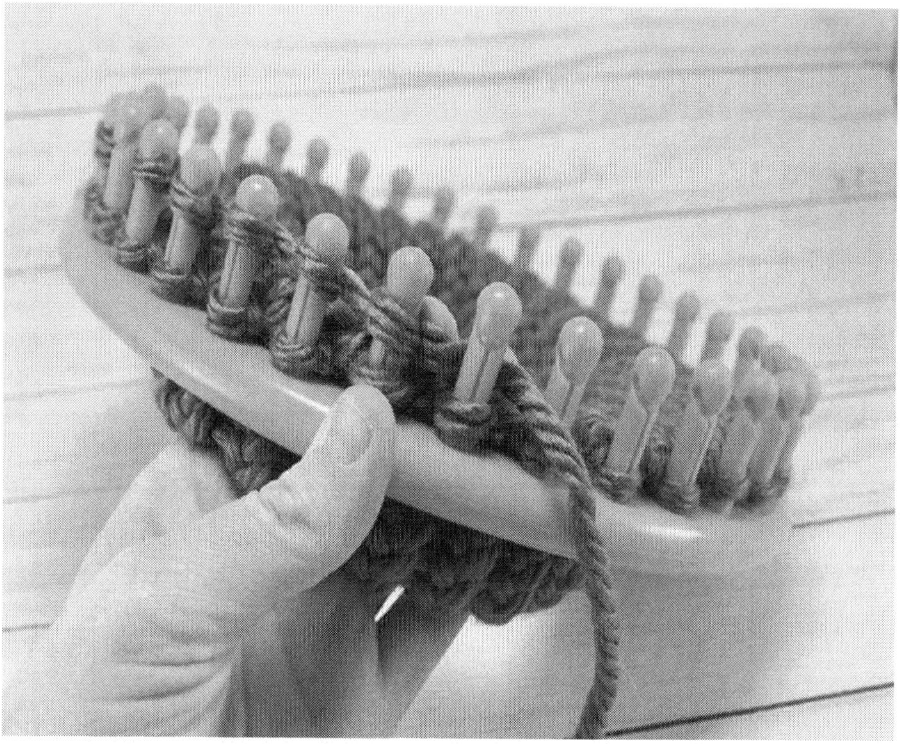

After that just continue knitting as you please!

I really love how making a brim is a thicker piece since it's doubled over. That added thickness makes for an awesome look. It also eliminates how the bottom of knit caps like to roll up like the one I made below.

The brim also adds extra warmth with 2 layers instead of just the 1 and it also adds more protection against the wind which is perfect for anyone who suffers frequent earaches.

So there you have it. Easy peasy loom knit hats with a brim!

Made in the USA
Middletown, DE
04 March 2022

62149623R00035